365 Provocative Questions for Young Men Aged 18-19

365 Provocative Questions for Young Men Aged 18-19

One Question a Day to Forge Independence and Shape Their Future

Aria Capri Publishing
Devon Abbruzzese
Mauricio Vasquez

Toronto, Canada

365 Provocative Questions for Young Men Aged 18-19 by Aria Capri Publishing [Aria Capri International Inc.]. All Rights Reserved.

All rights reserved. No part of this publication may be reproduced, distributed, shared with third parties, stored in any type of retrieval system, digitized, or transmitted in any form or by any means, including but not limited to electronic, mechanical, photocopying, recording, or otherwise, without the prior written permission of the publisher. Unauthorized reproduction or distribution of this publication, or any portion of it, may result in severe civil and criminal penalties and will be prosecuted to the fullest extent permitted by law.

Copyright © 2024, Aria Capri Publishing [Aria Capri International Inc.]. All Rights Reserved.

<u>Authors:</u>
Devon Abbruzzese
Mauricio Vasquez
Aria Capri Publishing

First Printing: May 2024

ISBN-978-1-998402-49-6 (Paperback book)
ISBN-978-1-998402-48-9 (Hardcover book)
ISBN-978-1-998402-47-2 (Electronic book)

Introduction

At the cusp of adulthood, young men aged 18 to 19 find themselves navigating a complex world filled with new responsibilities, shifting relationships, and evolving self-perceptions. This period, often marked by an intense exploration of identity and purpose, presents unique challenges and opportunities. As an author dedicated to adolescent development, I have come to recognize the profound impact that thoughtful, engaging questions can have on the growth and well-being of late adolescents. This book is crafted with the belief that the right questions can not only illuminate the path of personal growth but also strengthen the bonds between young men and those who care deeply about their development.

The Importance of Inquiry

Asking questions is fundamental to human interaction—it is how we learn about ourselves and the world around us. For late adolescent boys, who are on the brink of significant life decisions about careers, relationships, and personal values, the art of questioning can be particularly transformative. Questions encourage introspection and critical thinking, skills essential for successful navigation of adult life. They compel the young mind to explore boundaries of knowledge and experience, fostering resilience and adaptability.

Fostering Stronger Relationships

In the journey of late adolescence, the relationships that young men form with peers, family members, and mentors play a crucial role. Thoughtful questions open channels of communication and build trust. When parents and caregivers engage in meaningful dialogue through questions, they not only offer guidance but also demonstrate respect for the young person's emerging autonomy. This mutual exchange deepens understanding and nurtures a secure base from which the adolescent can confidently explore his evolving world.

Personal Growth Through Reflective Inquiry

The questions posed in this book are designed to prompt reflection on a variety of topics crucial to late adolescence—from career aspirations and relationships to personal values and emotional well-being. Each question serves as a stepping stone towards greater self-awareness and critical reflection, essential components of personal growth. By encouraging young men to articulate their thoughts and feelings, we help them build a coherent sense of self, which is pivotal during this transitional stage of life.

The Role of Caregivers and Mentors

This book also serves as a resource for those who play a supportive role in the lives of late adolescent boys—parents, teachers, coaches, and mentors. The act of asking insightful questions not only provides the young men with clarity and perspective but also empowers caregivers to be effective guides. It facilitates a deeper understanding of the young adult's needs and challenges, enabling more targeted and effective support.

A Call to Engage

As we delve into the questions in this book, it is my hope that they will spark curiosity, inspire dialogue, and promote a deeper connection with oneself and others. The transition from adolescence to adulthood is filled with potential; it is a time ripe for asking questions that challenge, motivate, and enlighten. By embracing the power of questions, we can help late adolescent boys not just to navigate but to thrive during these formative years.

This book is an invitation to explore the rich landscape of late adolescence through the lens of inquiry—a tool that, when used wisely, has the power to transform lives. Let us embark on this journey together, with open hearts and minds, ready to discover the profound impact that thoughtful questioning can have on the path to adulthood.

Let the journey of questions begin.

Devon & Mauricio

Scan the QR code to access the full collection

Guidelines for Asking Questions to Adolescents

Read the following guidelines to learn more about asking questions that unlock learning, foster communication and improve relationships.

- **Effective questions are open or focused, depending on the context**: Questions that open awareness and learning are open-ended questions that cannot be answered with a yes or no. Such questions evoke deeper thinking and reflection.
- **Effective questions support learning**: The goal is to stimulate thinking and deepen understanding of the situation. Insightful questions should focus attention on the most valuable aspects of the issue at hand, helping adolescents understand their experiences and feelings better.
- **Effective questions are asked for the benefit of others**: The intent is to stimulate the thinking and deepen the understanding of adolescents. It is not necessarily about the questioner and their needs.
- **Effective questions engage a personal response**: Engaging adolescents by inviting a personal response—how they feel, what emotions they are bringing to the situation—is crucial. The more a question invites a personal response to a challenge or choice, the more powerful it is for facilitating learning and growth.
- **Effective questions look beyond problems to future outcomes**: When adolescents are entangled in a problem, impactful questions shift the perspective from the problem to the solution, opening new opportunities for action and positive thinking.
- **Effective questions facilitate openness versus defensiveness**: Impactful questions are worded and expressed with a non-judgmental tone and open body language to prevent a defensive reaction. It is usually best to avoid questions that begin with "why" since they often elicit defensive responses or explanations.
- **Effective questions co-create best options versus manipulating outcomes**: Impactful questions are not intended to manipulate or lead adolescents to the option you might think is the best. If you want to suggest, it is best made directly as a suggestion versus a disguised directive through a question.
- **Less is more**: For questions, less is usually more. Ask only one question at a time and avoid long-winded, complicated questions.

Share Your Experience

Thank you for choosing this book. We hope this has provided meaningful insights and fostered valuable conversations for you and your child.

Your feedback helps us improve and helps other parents and young readers discover this resource. Reviews increase the book's visibility, making it easier for those who might benefit from its content to find it.

If you found this book helpful, please take a moment to leave a review by scanning this QR code.

Your experience can inspire and guide others on their journey of self-discovery and growth. We appreciate your support. Thank you.

Devon & Mauricio

Disclaimer

Dear Readers,

This book is designed to serve as a tool for personal growth, reflection, and exploring thoughts and feelings. The questions provided within these pages aim to inspire introspection and conversation, fostering a deeper understanding of oneself and the world.

However, it is important to understand that this book is not a substitute for professional advice, diagnosis, or treatment. While the questions can guide meaningful discussions and self-discovery, they are not intended to address or resolve serious issues or health concerns.

If you or your child encounters significant emotional, psychological, or physical challenges, we strongly recommend seeking the guidance of a qualified professional. This may include consulting a doctor, mental health professional, counselor, or any other relevant specialist who can provide the appropriate support and interventions.

The publisher, author, and any associated parties take no responsibility for any consequences resulting from the use of this book. It is up to the reader to exercise their judgment and discretion when engaging with the questions and interpreting their answers. The insights and reflections gained from this book should be seen as a starting point for further exploration and, when necessary, professional consultation.

We hope that this book serves as a valuable resource for personal growth and development. Remember, each individual's journey of self-discovery is unique, and seeking help when needed is a sign of strength and wisdom.

Day 1
How do you feel about the physical changes your body has undergone during puberty?

Day 2
What are some ways you prefer to exercise, and how often do you find time for physical activity?

Day 3
How does your current diet reflect your understanding of nutrition and health?

Day 4
Can you describe a time when you successfully managed a stressful situation?

Day 5
What qualities do you value most in a friend and why?

Day 6
How has your relationship with your family evolved as you've grown older?

Day 7
What role does social media play in your life? Do you feel it impacts your self-esteem?

Day 8
How do you approach problem-solving in your schoolwork or other areas of life?

Day 9
Reflect on how you've used reading and writing skills in a practical situation recently.

Day 10
What learning style do you find most effective for you, and how do you incorporate it into your study habits?

Day 11
Looking back, what cognitive milestones do you feel you've achieved in the last year?

Day 12
How have your language skills helped you express yourself better?

Day 13
What strategies do you use to manage feelings like stress or anxiety?

Day 14
Reflect on a moment when you felt very resilient. What helped you bounce back?

Day 15
How aware are you of conditions like depression or anxiety in yourself or others?

Day 16
How do your cultural background and family values influence your decision-making?

Day 17

What impact do you think the media has on your views and behaviors?

Day 18

How does your socioeconomic background affect your access to opportunities?

Day 19

What measures do you take to ensure your physical safety in daily life?

Day 20

How do you maintain emotional safety in your relationships?

Day 21
Are there particular online safety practices you follow to protect your privacy and well-being?

Day 22
Can you discuss a moral dilemma you've faced and how you resolved it?

Day 23
In what ways do you explore or express your spiritual beliefs and values?

Day 24
How often do you get to spend time in natural settings, and what does this mean to you?

Day 25
Describe the differences you notice in lifestyle between urban and rural settings based on your experiences.

Day 26
How do you define self-esteem, and what factors most influence yours?

Day 27
When do you feel most empathetic, and how do you show it in your actions?

Day 28
Can you describe a moment when understanding another person's feelings deeply affected you?

Day 29
What are the top three traits you believe every leader should have?

Day 30
How do you handle conflicts with peers, and what do you think works best for resolving them?

Day 31
In what ways do you contribute to your family's emotional dynamics?

Day 32
How do you think your education has prepared you for the real world?

Day 33
What are some key achievements in your education that you're particularly proud of?

Day 34
How do you deal with distractions when you need to focus on your studies or tasks?

Day 35
What are your main goals for the next five years, and how do you plan to achieve them?

Day 36
How has your understanding of right and wrong evolved as you've grown older?

Day 37
What does mental health mean to you, and how do you maintain yours?

Day 38
Reflect on how your friendships have changed over the past few years. What have you learned from these changes?

Day 39
What does it mean to you to be independent, and how are you working towards that?

Day 40
How do you balance your use of digital devices with other aspects of your life?

Day 41
When do you feel most confident about yourself, and what activities are you doing at those times?

Day 42
How have your goals and aspirations changed over the past year?

Day 43
What's one new hobby or skill you'd like to learn this year, and why?

Day 44
Can you describe a time when you had to overcome a significant challenge on your own?

Day 45
How does engaging with digital media and social networks influence your self-esteem?

Day 46
In what ways do you contribute to your family's emotional environment?

Day 47
How do you approach conflicts within your family or with close friends?

Day 48
What are your thoughts on the importance of teamwork, both in sports and in academic settings?

Day 49
How do you manage stress from school or work, and what methods have you found most effective?

Day 50
Can you identify a moment when you felt a strong sense of empathy towards someone else? What triggered it?

Day 51
What qualities do you look for in a friend, and how do you nurture those relationships?

Day 52
How has your understanding of physical health evolved as you've grown older?

Day 53
What strategies do you use to ensure you're eating a balanced and nutritious diet?

Day 54
How do you feel about your personal safety when navigating online spaces?

Day 55
Can you discuss a time when you felt misunderstood by others? How did you handle the situation?

Day 56
What are your strategies for dealing with peer pressure, especially in situations that test your values?

Day 57
How do you balance school responsibilities with personal interests and hobbies?

Day 58
What role do you think physical activity plays in your overall mental health?

Day 59
Have you ever had to advocate for yourself or someone else? What was the situation, and what did you do?

Day 60
What are your thoughts on the relationship between mental health and academic performance?

Day 61
How do you define success in your personal life and your academic or career paths?

Day 62
What are your views on the importance of cultural identity and heritage in shaping who you are?

Day 63
How do you manage your time between technology usage and face-to-face interactions with people?

Day 64
What's one thing you wish adults understood better about people your age?

Day 65
How do you react when you encounter failure, and what steps do you take to move forward?

Day 66
In what ways do you think being a part of a community contributes to your personal growth?

Day 67
How do you approach learning about new cultures and viewpoints different from your own?

Day 68
What are some effective ways you've found to manage and alleviate feelings of anxiety?

Day 69
Can you identify a person who has been a positive influence in your life? What qualities do they possess that you admire?

Day 70
How do you navigate the challenges of maintaining privacy while being active on social media?

Day 71
What steps do you take to stay informed about current events, and why do you think it's important?

Day 72
How do you think your life experiences differ from those of your parents at your age?

Day 73
Can you describe a recent situation where you had to use problem-solving skills to overcome a difficulty?

Day 74
What are your thoughts on the balance between individuality and conforming to social norms?

Day 75
How do you plan to finance your further education or career training?

Day 76
What role does creativity play in your life, and how do you express it?

Day 77
How do you handle the pressure of making decisions that can impact your long-term future?

Day 78
Can you identify a personal belief or value that has changed recently? What influenced this change?

Day 79
How do you maintain emotional safety in your relationships, and why is it important?

Day 80
What are your strategies for dealing with disappointment or setbacks?

Day 81
How do you ensure that you make time for relaxation and leisure, and why is this important?

Day 82
How has your understanding of ethics and morality developed through your teenage years?

Day 83
What do you think are the most significant challenges faced by your generation?

Day 84
How do you approach responsibilities at home, such as chores or caring for siblings?

Day 85
What are your thoughts on lifelong learning and self-improvement?

Day 86
How do you deal with changes in your friendships as you grow older?

Day 87
What measures do you take to ensure your physical health is a priority?

Day 88
How do you balance your personal desires with the expectations of your family or society?

Day 89
What has been the most impactful piece of advice you've received, and who gave it to you?

Day 90
How do you approach conflicts when your values are challenged by others?

Day 91
What has been your biggest realization about yourself this year?

Day 92
How do you manage the stress that comes with academic or career planning?

Day 93
What are your plans for contributing to your community or making a difference in the world?

Day 94
How do you stay motivated when you face obstacles in your goals?

Day 95
Can you share a time when you had to stand up for what you believe was right?

Day 96
How do you foster a positive self-image amid societal pressures and expectations?

Day 97
What steps do you take to cultivate a healthy lifestyle, including sleep, diet, and exercise?

Day 98
How do you prioritize tasks and manage your time effectively?

Day 99
What are your methods for coping with anxiety about the future?

Day 100
How do you think your personal and professional identities are evolving?

Day 101
How do you approach making new friendships that align with your values and interests?

Day 102
What are your strategies for maintaining focus and concentration during demanding tasks?

Day 103
How do you navigate your relationship with technology in a way that benefits your mental health?

Day 104
What role does forgiveness play in your relationships?

Day 105
How do you decide when it's appropriate to seek help from others?

Day 106
What are the key factors you consider when setting personal goals?

Day 107
How do you approach discussions about difficult topics with your peers or family?

Day 108
What are your views on the importance of resilience in achieving personal success?

Day 109
How do you assess the credibility of information you find online?

Day 110
What has been a significant turning point in your development of self-awareness?

Day 111
How do you feel about your future, and what steps are you taking to shape it?

Day 112
What practices do you find most effective for managing your emotions during stressful times?

Day 113
How do you balance listening to advice and making your own decisions?

Day 114
What are your thoughts on the role of physical activities in building character?

Day 115
How do you approach resolving conflicts that arise in online settings?

Day 116
What actions do you take to secure your privacy and personal data online?

Day 117
How do you think about and plan for your physical safety in different environments?

Day 118
What steps do you take to build and maintain trust in your relationships?

Day 119
How do you respond when someone challenges your beliefs or opinions?

Day 120
In what ways do you think your upbringing has shaped your current worldview and personality?

Day 121
What inspires you to learn and how do you apply your knowledge in daily life?

Day 122
How do you differentiate between healthy and unhealthy competition?

Day 123
What personal milestones are you looking forward to achieving this year?

Day 124
Can you describe a situation where you had to advocate for your own health or well-being?

Day 125
How do you define personal success, and how has this definition changed over time?

Day 126
What kind of legacy would you like to leave through your actions and choices?

Day 127
How do you stay true to your values when faced with societal pressures?

Day 128
What are some ways you contribute to a positive environment in your school or workplace?

Day 129
How do you prepare yourself to adapt to major life changes?

Day 130
Can you discuss a recent act of kindness you observed or participated in?

Day 131
How do you handle feelings of jealousy or envy when they arise?

Day 132
What role do mentors or role models play in your life, and how do you interact with them?

Day 133
How do you navigate the challenges of saving and spending money wisely?

Day 134
What are your strategies for staying calm and focused under pressure?

Day 135
How do you approach problem-solving when faced with a difficult decision?

Day 136
What activities help you reconnect with yourself when you feel out of balance?

Day 137
How do you approach forgiveness, both giving and receiving?

Day 138
What steps are you taking to develop leadership skills?

Day 139
How do you address misunderstandings with friends or family to clear up conflicts?

Day 140
What have you learned about yourself through your relationships with others?

Day 141
How do you balance the need for independence with the benefits of seeking advice?

Day 142
What are your thoughts on the importance of community service?

Day 143
How do you deal with the fear of failure when trying something new?

Day 144
What techniques do you use to enhance your memory and learning skills?

Day 145
How do you maintain motivation for subjects or tasks that don't immediately interest you?

Day 146
What are the most important factors you consider when planning your career path?

Day 147
How do you ensure that you are respectful of differing opinions in a discussion?

Day 148
What practices help you maintain mental clarity and emotional stability?

Day 149
How do you assess your own strengths and weaknesses, and how does this influence your goals?

Day 150
What steps do you take to ensure you're building healthy and supportive friendships?

Day 151
How do you deal with criticism, both constructive and otherwise?

Day 152
What has been the most challenging aspect of your education so far?

Day 153
How do you ensure that you are making ethical decisions, especially in complex situations?

Day 154
What role does gratitude play in your life, and how do you express it?

Day 155
How do you stay informed and critical of the media you consume?

Day 156
How do you balance the desire for personal achievement with the needs of your community or team?

Day 157
What actions do you take to stay safe online and protect your digital identity?

Day 158
How has your relationship with your family evolved as you've moved towards adulthood?

Day 159
What are your strategies for coping with rejection, whether in personal or professional contexts?

Day 160
How do you prioritize and manage your responsibilities effectively?

Day 161
How do you nurture your spiritual or philosophical beliefs, and how do they impact your daily actions?

Day 162
What are the most valuable lessons you've learned from sports or other physical activities?

Day 163
How do you approach setting realistic yet challenging goals for yourself?

Day 164
What methods do you use to stay connected with your cultural heritage?

Day 165
How do you think your personal experiences have shaped your views on teamwork and collaboration?

Day 166
What do you think are the key elements of a successful and fulfilling relationship?

Day 167
How do you find balance between using technology productively and avoiding its overuse?

Day 168
What measures do you take to cultivate a positive and optimistic outlook on life?

Day 169

How do you approach learning about and respecting diverse perspectives and cultures?

Day 170

What new skill or hobby would you like to explore next, and why?

Day 171

What strategies do you employ to manage time effectively when juggling multiple responsibilities?

Day 172

How do you approach making new friends in unfamiliar settings?

Day 173
What aspects of your cultural background are you most proud of, and how do they shape your identity?

Day 174
How do you determine what information online is trustworthy?

Day 175
What are some ways you show support to friends going through tough times?

Day 176
How do you define emotional strength, and who in your life embodies this trait?

Day 177
In what ways do you contribute to discussions and decisions in your family?

Day 178
What are the most significant pressures you face from social media, and how do you handle them?

Day 179
How do you prepare yourself mentally and physically before a big event, like an exam or a sports competition?

Day 180
What is your approach to balancing work and relaxation during your weekends?

Day 181
How do you deal with the feeling of being overwhelmed by expectations—either your own or others'?

Day 182
What are your main considerations when planning for your financial future?

Day 183
How do you maintain a positive outlook during times of uncertainty?

Day 184
What personal traits do you think are most important for leadership?

Day 185
How do you determine which of your passions to pursue more seriously?

Day 186
What steps do you take to stay healthy during the cold and flu season?

Day 187
How do you approach ethical dilemmas, and can you give an example of such a situation?

Day 188
What methods do you use to reduce stress before it affects your health or mood?

Day 189
How do you maintain your personal integrity in different social situations?

Day 190
What role does self-reflection play in your personal development?

Day 191
How do you respond when you realize you've made a mistake?

Day 192
What have you learned about yourself from a recent failure?

Day 193
How do you decide when it's necessary to end a friendship that isn't beneficial to you?

Day 194
What are your thoughts on the importance of self-discipline, and how do you cultivate it?

Day 195
How do you evaluate the success of a day or a project? What criteria do you use?

Day 196
How do you handle situations where you have to work with someone you don't get along with?

Day 197
What are the most important factors you consider when making career choices?

Day 198
How do you approach learning from people who are different from you?

Day 199
What actions do you take to protect your mental health when using social media?

Day 200
How do you approach resolving misunderstandings that arise in digital communications?

Day 201
How do you prioritize your personal values when making decisions?

Day 202
What are the benefits of having a diverse group of friends, and how does this diversity affect your perspectives?

Day 203
How do you maintain your focus and motivation during a long-term project or goal?

Day 204
What are your strategies for effective communication in relationships?

Day 205
How do you ensure that you are continually growing and learning?

Day 206
What are your methods for coping with loneliness or isolation?

Day 207
How do you decide when to ask for help, and whom do you approach?

Day 208
What has been your most memorable travel experience, and what did you learn from it?

Day 209
How do you ensure fairness in your interactions with others?

Day 210
How do you negotiate compromises in situations with conflicting interests?

Day 211
What role do hobbies play in your life, and how do they contribute to your happiness?

Day 212
How do you maintain balance between personal life and educational/career aspirations?

Day 213
What steps do you take to understand and manage your emotions during stressful times?

Day 214
How do you react when confronted with unexpected challenges or changes?

Day 215
What are your thoughts on the impact of volunteering on personal growth?

Day 216
How do you assess the role of persistence in achieving your goals?

Day 217
How do you handle the pressure to conform to certain behaviors or trends?

Day 218
What practices do you find most helpful in maintaining a healthy body image?

Day 219
How do you cultivate patience in situations where immediate results are not possible?

Day 220
What are some ways you seek to understand and improve your weaknesses?

Day 221
What strategies do you use to keep yourself organized with school and personal tasks?

Day 222
How do you determine the credibility of sources when researching information for school projects or personal interest?

Day 223
What role does gratitude play in your daily life, and how do you practice it?

Day 224
How do you approach setting boundaries in relationships, and why are they important?

Day 225
What aspects of your life give you the most happiness and fulfillment?

Day 226
How do you handle situations where you feel out of your depth?

Day 227
What are your strategies for maintaining mental wellness during high-stress periods?

Day 228
How do you measure personal growth, and what benchmarks do you use?

Day 229
What steps do you take to ensure that you are respectful and inclusive in your interactions with others?

Day 230
How do you approach discussing your future career plans with your parents or guardians?

Day 231
What are your thoughts on the importance of adaptability in today's world?

Day 232
How do you stay motivated to pursue your goals when progress seems slow?

Day 233
What has been your most effective method for learning new skills?

Day 234
How do you manage your time when balancing multiple interests and commitments?

Day 235
How do you ensure that you are making environmentally conscious choices?

Day 236
What role does creativity play in your academic or career pursuits?

Day 237
How do you handle disagreements in viewpoints with people you respect?

Day 238
What methods do you use to deal with rejection, whether personal or professional?

Day 239
How do you decide which responsibilities to prioritize on a busy day?

Day 240
What are your thoughts on the impact of positive thinking on personal outcomes?

Day 241
How do you navigate the stress associated with major life decisions?

Day 242
What experiences have taught you the most about yourself?

Day 243
How do you stay connected with friends and family amidst a busy schedule?

Day 244
What role do personal projects or hobbies play in your life?

Day 245
How do you approach the challenge of maintaining a healthy work-life balance?

Day 246
What has been your biggest challenge in managing your own health and wellness?

Day 247
How do you approach learning from mistakes, both yours and others'?

Day 248
What are your strategies for building resilience against everyday stresses?

Day 249
How do you handle peer pressure when it conflicts with your personal values?

Day 250
What importance do you place on having a mentor, and what qualities do you look for in one?

Day 251
How do you approach making sacrifices for the greater good or for long-term benefits?

Day 252
What steps do you take to maintain your focus during long study sessions or projects?

Day 253
How do you determine when it's time to step out of your comfort zone?

Day 254
What has been your experience with teamwork in both positive and challenging situations?

Day 255
How do you assess the balance between digital life and real-world interactions?

Day 256
What have you learned about leadership from your own experiences in leadership roles?

Day 257
How do you handle the pressure of societal expectations regarding success and achievement?

Day 258
What measures do you take to stay safe when engaging in physical activities or sports?

Day 259
How do you deal with the challenges of self-doubt and insecurity?

Day 260
What are your methods for managing distractions while working on important tasks?

Day 261
How do you build trust in new relationships?

Day 262
What are the most important factors you consider when planning for your educational future?

Day 263
How do you handle feelings of frustration when things don't go as planned?

Day 264
What are your strategies for effective stress relief that have proven successful for you?

Day 265
How do you approach conversations about sensitive topics with peers or adults?

Day 266
What methods do you use to reflect on your personal achievements and areas for improvement?

Day 267
How do you plan to ensure that your career or academic choices align with your long-term goals?

Day 268
What lessons have you learned about collaboration from group projects or team sports?

Day 269
How do you ensure that you are contributing positively to your community?

Day 270
How do you manage the expectations set by your family, friends, and yourself?

Day 271
What strategies do you use to remain patient when progress in your personal goals seems slow?

Day 272
How do you determine the reliability of news sources, and why is this important?

Day 273
What are some ways you can demonstrate leadership without holding an official position?

Day 274
How do you handle situations where you feel misunderstood by others?

Day 275
What are your thoughts on the importance of self-care, and how do you practice it?

Day 276
How do you maintain enthusiasm for projects or tasks over long periods?

Day 277
What steps do you take to prepare for a significant transition, such as going to college or starting a job?

Day 278
How do you handle the pressure to meet the expectations of others, particularly your family?

Day 279
What are the benefits of having a routine, and how do you maintain one?

Day 280
How do you approach making new friends who share your values and interests?

Day 281
What are your strategies for staying engaged in subjects or activities that you find challenging?

Day 282
How do you address feelings of loneliness or isolation?

Day 283
What methods do you find most effective for resolving conflicts with someone close to you?

Day 284
How do you balance the need for personal space with family obligations?

Day 285
What are your methods for staying informed about global events and their implications?

Day 286
How do you approach decision-making when faced with ethical dilemmas?

Day 287
What steps do you take to develop and maintain a positive outlook in life?

Day 288
How do you manage and prioritize your mental health in a busy lifestyle?

Day 289
What are your strategies for dealing with the anxiety of uncertain outcomes?

Day 290
How do you foster and maintain a sense of curiosity and a desire to learn?

Day 291
What experiences have you had that shaped your understanding of friendship?

Day 292
How do you approach self-improvement in areas you find personally challenging?

Day 293
What importance do you place on physical fitness, and how do you incorporate it into your routine?

Day 294
How do you assess the impact of your actions on your community and environment?

Day 295
What measures do you take to protect your personal information online?

Day 296
How do you stay motivated to maintain healthy eating habits?

Day 297
What are the key factors that influence your voting decisions or political opinions?

Day 298
How do you negotiate personal boundaries in a digital world?

Day 299
What are some ways you can contribute to a sustainable future?

Day 300
How do you manage the balance between taking risks and maintaining safety?

Day 301
What role does forgiveness play in your personal relationships?

Day 302
How do you handle criticism and use it to your advantage?

Day 303
What are the most valuable lessons you've learned from your elders?

Day 304
How do you approach learning from different cultures and experiences?

Day 305
What methods do you use to cope with the pressures of academic or career performance?

Day 306
How do you deal with feelings of inadequacy or comparing yourself to others?

Day 307
What steps do you take to cultivate empathy towards others?

Day 308
How do you decide when it's time to make a significant change in your life?

Day 309
What are your thoughts on the importance of artistic expression, and how do you engage with art?

Day 310
How do you prioritize which social issues to be informed about or active in?

Day 311
What role do personal failures play in your overall growth and development?

Day 312
How do you ensure that your goals align with your long-term vision for your life?

Day 313
What strategies do you use to manage stress during critical exams or interviews?

Day 314
How do you approach maintaining a balance between individuality and community expectations?

Day 315
What are some effective ways you've found to manage your time during busy periods?

Day 316
How do you approach building and maintaining trust in your personal and professional relationships?

Day 317
What has been your approach to handling heartbreak or emotional distress?

Day 318
How do you balance your aspirations with the practical aspects of your life?

Day 319
What are your strategies for engaging with people who have different viewpoints without causing conflict?

Day 320
How do you handle the transition from being a student to entering the workforce or higher education?

Day 321
How do you evaluate your personal growth at the end of each year?

Day 322
What are some ways you express gratitude towards others, and why do you think it's important?

Day 323
How do you approach disagreements on social or political issues with friends?

Day 324
What techniques do you use to enhance your focus and attention during tasks that require high concentration?

Day 325
How do you maintain a sense of calm and composure in unexpected or stressful situations?

Day 326
What are the key factors you consider when making plans for your physical and mental well-being?

Day 327
How do you ensure that your actions reflect your personal values and ethics?

Day 328
What role does mentorship play in your personal and professional development?

Day 329
How do you approach setting and achieving goals that seem ambitious or challenging?

Day 330
What steps do you take to stay motivated and inspired in your hobbies or interests?

Day 331
How do you deal with the challenge of maintaining long-distance friendships?

Day 332
What practices help you stay grounded and present in your daily life?

Day 333
How do you manage your energy levels throughout a busy day?

Day 334
What strategies do you find effective for calming your mind before bedtime?

Day 335
How do you approach conversations about your future plans with those who may have different expectations for you?

Day 336
What steps do you take to develop your problem-solving skills?

Day 337
How do you manage the balance between learning from others and maintaining your own point of view?

Day 338
What actions do you take to improve your resilience in the face of setbacks?

Day 339
How do you determine which aspects of your life need more attention or improvement?

Day 340
What techniques do you use to deal with procrastination?

Day 341
How do you handle the stress of balancing academic or work responsibilities with your social life?

Day 342
What methods do you use to ensure you are approachable in social situations?

Day 343
How do you cultivate a supportive network of friends and acquaintances?

Day 344
What are your strategies for dealing with the pressure to succeed from peers or family?

Day 345
How do you maintain your individuality while adapting to group dynamics?

Day 346
What has been the most significant adjustment you've made in your approach to learning?

Day 347
How do you approach making lifestyle changes that promote better health?

Day 348
What measures do you take to protect your emotional well-being when facing online negativity or criticism?

Day 349
How do you determine the right balance between saving and spending?

Day 350
What are some ways you actively listen and ensure others feel heard?

Day 351
How do you address your own biases or misconceptions?

Day 352
What strategies do you employ to enhance your creativity and innovation?

Day 353
How do you prioritize tasks when everything seems urgent?

Day 354
What methods do you use to recover from physical or emotional exhaustion?

Day 355
How do you navigate the complexities of modern relationships?

Day 356
What role does self-discipline play in your personal success?

Day 357
How do you cultivate patience and understanding in your interactions with others?

Day 358
What steps do you take to build confidence in areas where you feel insecure?

Day 359
How do you manage the expectations you set for yourself?

Day 360
What actions do you take to remain informed about your rights and responsibilities as a citizen?

Day 361
How do you approach decision-making when faced with uncertainty about the outcomes?

Day 362
What practices do you find helpful in maintaining a positive and realistic self-image?

Day 363
How do you ensure you make time for both personal reflection and social interaction?

Day 364
What has been a pivotal moment in your understanding of your own emotional needs?

Day 365

How do you celebrate your achievements and reflect on your growth over the past year?

Share Your Experience

Thank you for choosing this book. We hope this has provided meaningful insights and fostered valuable conversations for you and your child.

Your feedback helps us improve and helps other parents and young readers discover this resource. Reviews increase the book's visibility, making it easier for those who might benefit from its content to find it.

If you found this book helpful, please take a moment to leave a review by scanning this QR code.

Your experience can inspire and guide others on their journey of self-discovery and growth. We appreciate your support. Thank you.

Devon & Mauricio

www.ingramcontent.com/pod-product-compliance
Lightning Source LLC
Chambersburg PA
CBHW060415010526
44107CB00006B/702